5 STEPS
TO
CHRISTIAN
GROWTH

STUDY GUIDE

Bill Bright

CAMPUS CRUSADE FOR CHRIST

Building Spiritual Movements Everywhere

Five Steps to Christian Growth:
Study Guide

Published by
Campus Crusade for Christ/Bright Media Foundation
375 Highway 74 South, Suite A
Peachtree City, GA 30269

Written by Bill Bright. © 2007 Bright Media Foundation and Campus Crusade for
Christ, Inc. Previously © 1983-2002 CCC. All rights reserved. No part of this booklet
may be changed in any way or reproduced in any form or stored or transmitted by
computer or electronic means without written permission from Campus Crusade for
Christ. Published by Campus Crusade for Christ, 375 Highway 74 S., Suite A, Peachtree
City, GA. Printed in the United States of America.

Printed in the United States of America

ISBN: 1–56399-021–0

Distributed in Canada by Campus Crusade for Christ of Canada, Langley, B.C.

Unless otherwise indicated, all Scripture references are taken from the *New
International Version*, © 1973, 1978, 1984 by the International Bible Society.
Published by Zondervan Bible Publishers, Grand Rapids, Michigan.

Scripture quotations designated TLB are from *The Living Bible*, © 1971 by
Tyndale House Publishers, Wheaton, Illinois.

Scripture quotations designated NASB are from the *New American Standard
Bible*, © 1960, 1962, 1963, 1968, 1971, 1972, 1973, 1975, 1977 by the
Lockman Foundation, La Habra, California.

> Any royalties from this book or the many other books by Bill Bright are
> dedicated to the glory of God and designated to the various ministries of
> Campus Crusade for Christ.

Additional Materials Are Available for Christian Growth
If after completing this study you have come to know Christ personally or
would like further help in getting to know Christ better, two sites are
recommended:
www.startingwithGod.com or www.growinginChrist.com

If you still have questions, visit:
www.whoisJesus-really.com or www.everystudent.com

For a complete list of materials by Dr. Bright, including the *Ten Basic Steps*
and the *Transferable Concepts,* and other Bible study materials from Campus
Crusade for Christ, visit: www.campuscrusade.org or call 1-800-827-2788.

Contents

Acknowledgments

Through the years, I have written many books and hundreds of articles. In the beginning years of my ministry, I personally researched, wrote, edited, and polished each book manuscript and article.

Today, however, my responsibilities of leading a large worldwide movement and my appointments and travel schedule do not allow me such luxury.

In need of help, I happily sought the assistance of my good friend and editor, Don Tanner, and his staff of NewLife Publications to help me revise *Five Steps to Christian Growth.*

A special thanks to Don for his professional assistance and to Joette Whims for joining Don and me in the editorial process.

A Personal Word

When I am alone with a person for a few minutes, I assume that I am there by divine appointment.

Shortly before midnight a few nights ago, a call came to my unlisted number. When the man on the line realized he had misdialed, he began to apologize. "I'm sorry, sir," he said, "I have a wrong number. I'm trying to call my wife. I dialed you by mistake."

"No," I quickly assured him. "It's no mistake. God has a message for you. Would you like to hear it?"

"Yes!" he replied.

I explained how much God loves him and that God has a wonderful plan for his life. We talked for a few more moments during which I learned that he and his wife were having marital difficulties. Finally, I asked, "Are you a Christian?"

"No."

"Would you like to be?"

"Oh, yes. My mother and brother are both Christians, and I have wanted to receive Christ for a long time."

"Do you know how to receive Jesus Christ as your Savior?"

"No, I don't."

I explained very simply how he could receive Christ, then suggested he pray with me—phrase by phrase—to invite Jesus into his life. After we finished praying, he expressed great gratitude and joy. Later, I rushed materials to him for assurance and spiritual growth and also arranged for personal follow-up.

After thousands of similar privileges, I am convinced of one thing: at least 50 percent of all non-believers in your "Jerusalem" and throughout the world would receive Christ if properly approached by a trained Spirit--filled believer who can communicate God's love and forgiveness revealed through our Lord Jesus Christ.

If you, too, have a deep desire to introduce others to Jesus, I encourage you to receive training in how to share your faith. And begin every day with a prayer like this:

> Lord, lead me to someone today whose heart You have prepared to receive the joyful news of our loving Savior. Enable me to be Your messenger to show others how to find forgiveness of sin and the gift of eternal life. Amen.

As you rise from your knees and go out into your world to study or work, the Holy Spirit will honor that simple, earnest prayer and guide you to those whom He has prepared for your witness. As you meet people in the course of your day, ask the Lord, "Is it he? Is it she? Where is the person You want me to introduce to You?"

Always carry a *Four Spiritual Laws* booklet or a similar presentation so that when the "divine appointment" occurs and you recognize the opportunity, you can aggressively share your faith. Whether or not they receive Christ, leave them with the *Gospel of John*, *A Man Without Equal* book, the *Four Spiritual Laws*, or something similar to read.

This *Five Steps to Christian Growth* study is designed to train you to grow as a disciple and to live a godly life so you can share your faith in Christ more effectively. All you need is a desire to apply the biblical principles in these lessons to your life and a commitment to help others grow in Christ.

My prayer is that this study will bless and enrich your life and increase your effectiveness as a personal witness for our Lord. I assure you that there is no experience in life more exciting and spiritually rewarding than helping to introduce people to Christ.

Bill Bright

How You Can Be Sure You Are a Christian

The New Birth

Receiving Jesus Christ as Savior means experiencing a new, spiritual birth. Read John 3:1–8 and write a description of this new birth.

Our relationship with Christ involves three areas of commitment: intellect, emotions, and will. Which area creates the most problems for you?

Intellectual Commitment

Christianity is not a "blind" leap of faith, but a personal relationship with God through Jesus Christ. Read John 10:30–33 and 14:6–9.

How does Jesus' claim to be one with the Father ensure His ability to forgive sins?

What did each of the following people think about Jesus?

1. The apostle John (John 1:1, 14)

2. Thomas (John 20:25–28)

3. Jesus' enemies (John 5:18)

According to Romans 1:3, 4, what is the ultimate proof of Christ's claim to be God? How does this affect your life (verses 5, 6, 16, 17)?

The life that Jesus led, the miracles He performed, the words He spoke, His death on the cross, His resurrection, and His ascent to heaven all point to the fact that He was more than a mere man. What do the following verses tell us about who Jesus is and what He did for us?

1. Why did Jesus have to come to this earth? (Romans 3:23)

2. Why did Jesus die for us? (1 Peter 3:18)

3. What has Jesus Christ done for our sins that no one else can do? (1 Peter 2:24, 25)

4. Why is Christ's resurrection from the dead significant to us? (1 Peter 1:3)

Emotional Commitment

Seeking an emotional experience contradicts Hebrews 11:6. Faith is another word for trust. This trust must be placed in God and His Word rather than in what we feel. In what situations do you tend to trust in feelings rather than in God's Word?

1. What kind of experience did Paul have when he first met Jesus? (Acts 22:6–10)

2. What was Timothy's experience? (2 Timothy 1:5)

This diagram shows how we should let faith control our lives.

How can you let your faith control these situations? List specific ways you plan to do this.

Commitment of the Will

A commitment to Christ involves an act of the will. Although both mind and feelings are valid, you are not a Christian until, as an act of your will, you make a decision to receive Christ as your Savior and Lord. Have you taken this step? When?

The following are facts in which you can place your faith:

1. Christ came into your life. (Revelation 3:20)
• What does the door refer to?

• What does Christ promise?

• What is our part?

• What is His part?

• According to this verse, if you by faith open the door of your heart and invite Jesus Christ to come into your life to be your Savior and Lord, will He come in?

2. Your sins were forgiven. (Colossians 1:14)
• How many of your sins were forgiven?

• If God has forgiven you, why are there times when you are haunted by guilt feelings? (1 John 1:8, 9)

• What can be done about unconfessed sin?

3. You became a child of God. (John 1:12, 13)

• Who has been spiritually born into God's family?

• When you received Christ, what did you become?

4. You received eternal life. (1 John 5:11–13)

• According to this passage, who is the only One who can give us eternal life?

• Verse 13 says, "I write these things to you who believe in the name of the Son of God so that you may know that you have eternal life." According to Hebrews 13:5, if you have eternal life now, will it ever be taken away from you?

The Basis of Your Relationship with Christ

• What is the message of the gospel? (1 Corinthians 15:1–4)

• Why did Christ have to die? (1 Corinthians 15:3; Hebrews 9:22)

• What happens when a person responds to the gospel and receives Christ into his life? (John 1:12)

Our Confidence in Christ

If our relationship with God were dependent on our own good works, we could never have assurance of salvation. Read Ephesians 2:8, 9 and answer these questions:

• What is grace?

• In what are we to have faith? (See Galatians 3:22, 26.)

- On what basis did you obtain it?

- How do good works relate to your salvation?

- Why is boasting not acceptable?

Rewrite Ephesians 2:8, 9 and Galatians 3:22–26 in words you would use to explain the verses to a friend.

God's Promises to All Christians

What do these verses promise you as a result of your decision to trust in Christ?
- Revelation 3:20

- 1 John 5:11–13

- John 10:27–29

- John 5:24

Which promise is most meaningful to you? Why?

How can you apply these verses to strengthen your faith?

Action Point: This coming week, explain to a friend why you are sure you are a Christian.

How You Can Experience God's Love and Forgiveness

The Problem of Sin

1. Who has sinned? (Romans 3:23)

2. How did the sin of Adam, the father of the human race, affect you? (Romans 5:12)

3. What is the difference between temptation and sin?

• Who is the tempter? (Matthew 4:1)

• What causes you to be drawn into temptation? (James 1:13–15)

• How does sin differ from temptation?

13

What Is the Basis for Our Forgiveness?

1. According to John 1:29, what is Jesus called and what does He do?

Read Hebrews 10:1–18.

2. What did Jesus do for our sins?

Was this acceptable to God?

3. What did the sacrifice of Jesus accomplish for us?

4. How many of your sins did Christ forgive?

The Power of Sin

According to Romans 6:1–18, Christ not only died for our sin and forgave it, He also delivered us from sin's power.

1. What does God's Word tell you happened to your old sin nature when you became a Christian?

2. According to verse 11, what must you do?

3. According to verses 16 and 17, what choice faces you continuously?

4. What limit does God place on the temptations you face? (1 Corinthians 10:13)

5. What does God promise to provide you with when you are tempted?

Three Types of People

The Bible describes three types of people in 1 Corinthians, chapters 2 and 3. Underline the characteristics of each. Determine which type of life you are living.

• *The natural person* (1 Corinthians 2:14) is not a Christian. He depends on his own resources and lives in his own strength. Spiritually, he is dead to God—separated from God by sin.

Self-Directed Life
S – Self is on the throne
† – Christ is outside the life
● – Interests are directed by
     self, often resulting in
     discord and frustration

• *The spiritual person* (1 Corinthians 2:15, 16) is a Christian who is controlled and empowered by the Holy Spirit. He draws upon the unlimited resources of God's love and power and lives in the strength of the living Christ. He is alive to God because the Son of God is living in and through him. He brings glory to God because of his fruitful life and witness.

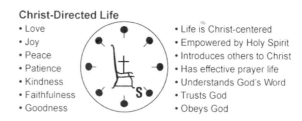

Christ-Directed Life
- Love
- Joy
- Peace
- Patience
- Kindness
- Faithfulness
- Goodness

- Life is Christ-centered
- Empowered by Holy Spirit
- Introduces others to Christ
- Has effective prayer life
- Understands God's Word
- Trusts God
- Obeys God

• *The worldly person* (1 Corinthians 3:1–3) is a believer trying to live the Christian life in his own strength. He is a defeated, fruitless Christian, who depends on his own abilities instead of drawing upon the inexhaustible resources of the Holy Spirit. He lives in frustration and slavery to sin (Romans 7:14–20).

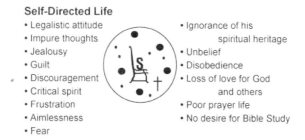

Self-Directed Life
- Legalistic attitude
- Impure thoughts
- Jealousy
- Guilt
- Discouragement
- Critical spirit
- Frustration
- Aimlessness
- Fear

- Ignorance of his
  spiritual heritage
- Unbelief
- Disobedience
- Loss of love for God
  and others
- Poor prayer life
- No desire for Bible Study

I am living the life of the _____ person.

Read Psalm 32:1–5.

1. What was King David's experience when he refused to confess his sins?

2. What happened when he acknowledged his sin?

Spiritual Breathing

A spiritual man lives by faith in God. Faith is trusting that God will do what He says He will do. When we place our faith in God and His Word, we can experience His love and power.

How can we get off the emotional, roller-coaster existence of a worldly life? By practicing "Spiritual Breathing," which is *exhaling* the impure (confessing our sins) and *inhaling* the pure (appropriating the power of the Holy Spirit as an act of our will by faith), 1 John 1:9; Ephesians 5:18.

Handling Guilt

When you feel guilty, compare your feelings to the criteria in this checklist, then circle the correct responses below. Follow the directions you have circled.

Checklist for Finding the Source of Guilt
When the Holy Spirit convicts me of sin: • He will point out a specific sin, and • God will forgive the sin and restore my fellowship with him as soon as I confess it. The guilt is immediately lifted. I am feeling false guilt if: • My feelings of guilt are vague and unspecific, or • I feel guilty over a sin that I previously and sincerely confessed to God.
Circle one: My feelings of guilt are (real) (false) so I will (exhale—confess it to God) (thank God that His forgiveness is immediate and complete).

Action Point: To *exhale*, follow these steps:

1. Ask the Lord to reveal any unconfessed sins. Write them on a piece of paper.
2. Confess these sins (agree with God that they are wrong).
3. Write 1 John 1:9 across the top. Destroy the list.
4. Make plans for restitution where you have wronged someone.

How You Can Be Filled With the Holy Spirit

Answer the following questions from the verses given.

Who Is the Holy Spirit?

- Acts 5:3, 4

- 1 Thessalonians 5:19; Ephesians 4:30

How do you know He is a person and not a force or impersonal power? 1 Corinthians 2:11; 12:11; Romans 15:30

- Matthew 28:19; 2 Corinthians 13:14

- What did Jesus call the Holy Spirit in John 14:16, 17?

Why Did the Holy Spirit Come?
- John 3:5

- John 16:7, 8, 13, 14

- John 7:37–39

- Acts 1:8

- Romans 8:26

- Ephesians 1:13, 14

What Does It Mean to Be Filled With the Spirit?

To be filled with the Spirit is to be filled with Jesus Christ, the risen Son of God, and to abide in Him. Since God is one shown through three persons, the Holy Spirit is the essence of Jesus. Filled means to be directed, controlled, and empowered by the Holy Spirit. When I am filled with the Spirit, Christ's Spirit will dwell in my body and live His resurrection life in and through me.

1. What is the difference between being filled with wine and being filled with the Spirit?

2. Why is a person different when he is filled with either one
    of these agents?

The Fruits of the Spirit

Read John 15:1–5, 8.

1. What comparison can you draw between the relationship
    of a vine to a branch and of Christ to a Christian?

2. What does "fruit" mean in verse 8?

How to Be Filled With the Holy Spirit

Although all Christians are indwelt by the Spirit, not all are
filled with the Spirit. Most Christians are not filled with the Spirit
because of:

- Lack of knowledge
- Unbelief

What is keeping you from being filled with the Spirit?

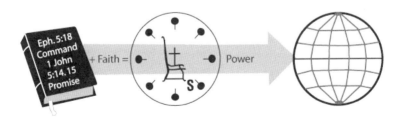

Action Point: To be filled with the Spirit, practice Spiritual Breathing.

Exhale:

• Ask the Holy Spirit to show you any unconfessed sin.

• Confess your sin and claim the promise of 1 John 1:9.

• Make restitution if necessary.

Inhale:

• Claim the filling of the Holy Spirit by faith on the basis of God's *command* and God's *promise* (Ephesians 5:18, 1 John 5:14, 15).

Here is a prayer you can use:

Dear Father, I need You. I acknowledge that I have been in control of my own life and have sinned against You. I thank You for forgiving my sins through Christ's death on the cross for me. I now invite Christ to take control of my life. Fill me with the Holy Spirit as You commanded me to be filled. You promised in Your Word that You would fill me if I ask in faith. As an expression of my faith, I now thank You for filling me with Your Holy Spirit and for taking control of my life. Amen.

How You Can Walk In the Spirit

As best you can, chart your spiritual well-being for the past few weeks, showing any "highs" or "lows" or steady progress you have made in applying Spiritual Breathing.

My Christian Walk

Perfect Success _____

Dismal Failure _____

Spiritual Conflict

Read Romans 7:14–25.

1. What was Paul's opinion of his flesh?

2. When we received Christ, in what new position were we placed in relation to Christ? (Ephesians 2:6)

3. What happened to us because of our position in Christ? (Romans 6:5, 6)

4. What happened to our old sin nature?

5. What must we do to have victory over the flesh?
*   Romans 6:11

*   Galatians 5:16, 17

Barriers to Walking in the Spirit

1. Barrier of Unconfessed Sin
    Sin will not affect our relationship with God; that is
permanent. Sin, however, will break our fellowship with God.
Match the statements on the left with the answers on the right.

A. Our relationship with God is:	1.Restored by confessing sin 2.Maintained by God 3.Capable of being broken 4.Maintained in part by us
B. Our fellowship with God is:	5.Eternally secure 6.Begun at salvation

Practicing Spiritual Breathing is a means to deal with
unconfessed sin. List the steps to Spiritual Breathing (refer to
Lesson 3).

1.

2.

3.

4.

2. Barrier of Self-Effort
    Read Romans 7:15–20.

1. What is the source of Paul's struggle in this passage?

2. How did that make him feel?

3. When have you experienced similar frustration?

3. Barrier of Circumstances
    Many Christians allow circumstances to sway their faith. But
we are to live by faith and believe in the trustworthiness of God's
Word. The train diagram illustrates the relationship between:
  • Fact (God and His Word)
  • Faith (our trust in God and His Word)
  • Feeling (the result of our faith and obedience)

    How can you be sure you are walking by faith rather than
feelings?

Dealing With Barriers

    List three areas of your life—such as dating, finances, or
family concerns—and describe how placing your faith in God's
Word would affect each circumstance.

    1.

2.

3.

Giving thanks is a practical way to demonstrate faith. Read the
verses and answer the following questions.
1. What does God promise in Romans 8:28?

2. What are we commanded to do in 1 Thessalonians 5:18?

3. Have you ever tried this in difficult circumstances? What
    happened?

4. What is a result of being filled with the Holy Spirit
    according to Ephesians 5:20?

Action Point: Whenever a circumstance or temptation
threatens to become a barrier between you and God this week,
review this chart and reaffirm your commitment to walk in the
Spirit.

Walking in the Spirit	Trusts in God and His Word	Experiences forgiveness through confession	Believes God in order to be filled with His Spirit	God causes growth and fruitfulness
Walking in Self-Effort	Trusts in self	Sin brings guilt or rationalization	Increased effort to live by God's standards	Frustration and defeat

How You Can Grow As a Christian

Read 2 Peter 3:18. What is the result of spiritual growth?

Principle One: We Must Read the Bible

1. Jesus said, "Man shall not live by bread alone." How did He say that we should live and be nourished? (Matthew 4:4)

2. The Bible is often referred to as "the Word of God" because it contains God's words to us. Why is reading God's Word so important? (2 Timothy 3:16, 17)

3. What will result in your life when you read God's Word? (Psalm 119:11, 105)

Principle Two: We Must Pray

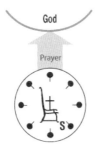

When praying, remember these things:
1. Pray about everything. (Philippians 4:6, 7)
   What is the result if we talk to God about everything?

2. Pray specifically. (John 14:14, 16:24)
   Why do you think it is important to pray specifically?

   What will be two results of praying specifically?

3. Pray continually. (1 Thessalonians 5:17)
   What does the Bible mean when it says to pray
   continually?

Principle Three: We Must Fellowship With Other Christians

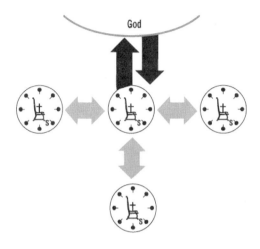

1. As God's children, what should we not neglect? (Hebrews 10:24, 25) Why?

2. What are the basic functions of a local church? (Colossians 1:25–28; 2 Timothy 4:2)

3. The new believers in the early church continued steadfastly in what four things? (Acts 2:41, 42)

    a.

    b.

   c.

   d.

4. If we spend 90 percent of our time with non-Christians and 10 percent with Christians, which group will have the greater influence on our lives? Why?

Principle Four: We Must Witness for Christ

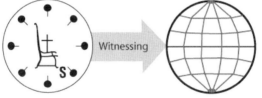

   One of the greatest acts of obedience is to share Christ with others in the power of the Holy Spirit. How did the first-century Christians obey the command to witness? Read Colossians 1:28, 29 and answer the questions.

1. What did Paul and the other believers do everywhere they went?

2. Why did they do this?

3. Where did they get the power to do this?

Romans 3:21–25 tells us what our message should be to those who do not know God personally. Read the verses from the *Living Bible*, then fill in the blanks.

1. In Romans 3:21, God says we cannot get to heaven by _____ or by trying to keep His _____.

2. Romans 3:23, 24 tell us that _____ have sinned and yet now God declares us not _____ if we _____ in Jesus Christ, who in His kindness freely takes away our _____.

3. Romans 3:25 says that God sent _____ to take the _____ for our sins and to end all God's anger against us. He used Christ's _____ and our _____ as the means of saving us from His wrath.

Answer the following questions.
1. What is the greatest thing that has ever happened to you?

2. What, then, is the greatest thing that you can do for another person?

3. In Romans 1:14–16, Paul tells us his own attitude about sharing the good news of Jesus Christ with others. Using his three "I's" as the keys to the passage, describe his attitude in your own words.

4. What was Jesus' promise in Acts 1:8?

Write down the names of several people with whom you plan to share your faith in Christ during the next week.

_____   _____

_____   _____

Principle Five: We Must Obey God

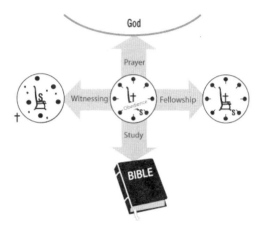

1. How can you prove that you love the Lord? (John 14:21)

2. What will be the result of keeping Christ's commandments? (John 15:10) What does that mean to you?

3. Where do we get the power to obey God? (Philippians 2:13)

4. In light of Christ's illustration in Luke 6:46–49, why would you say that obedience to Christ is imperative for your life?

Fill out the first chart to plan your quiet time for the next week. Use the second chart during your quiet time.

My Quiet Time With God							
Day	Sun.	Mon.	Tue.	Wed.	Thur.	Fri.	Sat.
Date							
Time							
Prayer requests							
Bible passage							

Specific Prayers Made	Date of Prayer	Date of Answer
1.		
2.		
3.		
4.		
5.		
6.		

How to Share Christ
With Others

A well-known Christian leader, highly gifted as a theologian, shared with me his frustration over his lack of effectiveness and fruitfulness in witnessing for Christ.

I asked him, "What do you say when you seek to introduce a person to Christ?"

He explained his presentation, which was long and complicated. The large number of Bible verses he used would confuse most people and prevent them from making an intelligent decision.

I challenged him to use the *Four Spiritual Laws* presentation daily for the next thirty days and report his progress to me at the end of that time.

When I saw him two weeks later, he was overflowing with joy and excitement. "By simply reading the booklet to others," he said, "I have seen more people come to Christ during the last two weeks than I had previously seen in many months. It's hard to believe!"

The *Four Spiritual Laws*[1] booklet, reproduced on pages 41 through 44, presents a clear and simple explanation of the gospel of our Lord Jesus Christ.

This booklet, available in all major languages of the world, has been developed as a result of more than forty years of experience in counseling with thousands of college students on campuses in almost every country on every continent in the world, as well as with a comparable number of laymen, pastors, and high school students. It represents one way to share your faith effectively.

---

[1] The *Four Spiritual Laws* booklet can be obtained by contacting Campus Crusade for Christ at 1-800-827-2788 or www.campuscrusade.org.

Benefits of *Four Laws*

Using a tool such as the *Four Spiritual Laws* offers many benefits. Let me list some of them:

• It enables you to open your conversation easily and naturally.

• It begins with a positive statement: "God loves you and has a wonderful plan for your life."

• It presents the gospel and the claims of Christ clearly and simply.

• It gives you confidence because you know what you are going to say and how you are going to say it.

• It enables you to be prepared at all times and to stick to the subject without getting off on tangents.

• It makes it possible for you to be brief and to the point.

• It enables you to lead others to a personal decision through a suggested prayer.

• It offers suggestions for growth, including the importance of involvement in the church.

• Of special importance, it is a "transferable tool" to give those whom you introduce to Christ so they can be encouraged and trained to lead others to Christ also. Paul exhorted Timothy, his young son in the faith:

The things you have heard me say in the presence of many witnesses entrust to reliable men who will also be qualified to teach others (2 Timothy 2:2).

The *Four Spiritual Laws* enables those who receive Christ to go immediately to friends and loved ones and tell them of their new-found faith in Christ. It also enables them to show their friends and loved ones how they, too, can make a commitment to Christ.

Various Approaches

You can introduce the *Four Spiritual Laws* to a non-believer. After a cordial, friendly greeting, you can use one of the following approaches:

• "I'm reading a little booklet that really makes sense to a lot of people. I'd like to share it with you. Have you heard of the *Four Spiritual Laws?*"

• "Do you ever think about spiritual things?" (Pause for an answer.) "Have you ever heard of the *Four Spiritual Laws?*"

• "A friend of mine recently gave me this little booklet that really makes sense to me. I would like to share it with you. Have you ever heard of the *Four Spiritual Laws?*"

• "The content of this booklet has been used to change the lives of millions of people. It contains truths that I believe will be of great interest to you. Would you read it and give me your impression?"

• "It is believed that this little booklet is the most widely printed piece of literature in the world apart from the Bible.[2] Would you be interested in reading it?"

Here is a direct approach that you can use when you have only a few moments with an individual:

• "If you died today, do you know for sure that you will go to heaven?"

If the answer is yes, ask:

• "On what do you base that knowledge? This little booklet, the *Four Spiritual Laws*, will help you know for sure that you will go to heaven when you die."

If the answer is no, say:

• "You can be sure you are going to heaven. This little booklet, the *Four Spiritual Laws*, tells how to know."

God will show you other ways to introduce this material. The important thing is to keep your introduction brief and to the point.

---

[2] It is estimated that over one-and-a-half billion *Four Spiritual Laws booklets* have been printed and distributed in all major languages of the world.

How to Present the
Four Spiritual Laws

1. Be sensitive to an individual's interest and the leading of the Holy Spirit. The simplest way to explain the *Four Spiritual Laws* is to read the booklet aloud to a non-believer. But be careful not to allow the presentation to become mechanical. Remember, you are not just sharing principles, you are introducing the person to Christ. The *Four Spiritual Laws* is simply a tool to help you effectively communicate the gospel. Pray for God's love to be expressed through you.

2. If there is any objection to the term "laws," use the term "Four Spiritual Principles" instead.[3]

3. When questions arise that would change the subject, explain that most questions are answered as you go through the *Four Spiritual Laws*. Or say, "That's a good question. Let's talk about it after we have completed reading the booklet."

4. Be sensitive to the individual. If he doesn't seem to respond, stop and ask, "Is this making sense?"

5. Hold the booklet so the individual can see it clearly. Use a pen to point to key areas. This will help hold his attention.

---

[3] You may want to use an adaptation of the *Four Spiritual Laws* entitled *Would You Like to Know God Personally?* It is available through Campus Crusade for Christ at 1-800-827-2788 or www.campuscrusade.org

6. In a group, give each person a *Four Spiritual Laws* booklet. Pray with those who are interested in receiving Christ. If only one is interested, be sensitive and in most cases talk with that person privately. Make sure each one understands that Christ comes into his life by faith. If he prays the prayer without believing Christ will answer, nothing will result.

Also be sensitive about whether he wants to pray his own prayer or use the prayer from the booklet. Some will request silent prayer.

7. If someone has already heard of the *Four Spiritual Laws*, ask him what he thought of them, and if he has any questions. If he is interested and the gospel is not clear to him, go over the booklet again.

8. When a person does not receive Christ when you first share the *Four Spiritual Laws* with him, make another appointment if he is interested. Give him the booklet *A Great Adventure* to take with him.(The booklet is available at your Christian bookstore or can be ordered through Campus Crusade for Christ.)

9. Pray for the person. Occasionally ask him if he has thought further about your discussion or if he has any questions.

10. Leave the *Four Spiritual Laws* or *A Great Adventure* with the person you have witnessed to whether or not he received Christ. Millions have received Christ through reading these booklets.

Have You Heard of the
Four Spiritual Laws?[*]

Just as there are physical laws that govern the physical universe, so are there spiritual laws that govern your relationship with God.

Law One
GOD **LOVES** YOU AND HAS A WONDERFUL **PLAN** FOR YOUR LIFE.

God's Love
"God so loved the world that He gave His only begotten Son, that whoever believes in Him should not perish, but have eternal life" (John 3:16).

God's Plan
[Christ speaking] "I came that they might have life, and might have it abundantly" [that it might be full and meaningful] (John 10:10).

Why is it that most people are not experiencing the abundant life?

Because...

Law Two
MAN IS **SINFUL** AND **SEPARATED** FROM GOD. THUS HE CANNOT KNOW AND EXPERIENCE GOD'S LOVE AND PLAN FOR HIS LIFE.

Man Is Sinful
"All have sinned and fall short of the glory of God" (Romans 3:23).

Man was created to have fellowship with God; but, because of his own stubborn self-will, he chose to go his own independent way and fellowship with God was broken. This self-will, characterized by an attitude of active rebellion or passive indifference, is an evidence of what the Bible calls sin.

Man Is Separated
"The wages of sin is death" [spiritual separation from God] (Romans 6:23).

---

[*] Note: All Scripture references are from the *New American Standard Bible*.

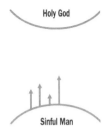

This diagram illustrates that God is holy and man is sinful. A great chasm separates the two. The arrows illustrate that man is continually trying to reach God and the abundant life through his own efforts: good life, ethics, philosophy, and more.

The Third Law gives us the only answer to this dilemma...

Law Three
JESUS CHRIST IS GOD'S **ONLY** PROVISION FOR MAN'S SIN. THROUGH HIM YOU CAN KNOW AND EXPERIENCE GOD'S LOVE AND PLAN FOR YOUR LIFE.

He Died In Our Place
"God demonstrates His own love toward us, in that while we were yet sinners, Christ died for us" (Romans 5:8).

He Rose from the Dead
"Christ died for our sins...He was buried...He was raised on the third day, according to the Scriptures...He appeared to Peter, then to the twelve. After that He appeared to more than five hundred..." (1 Corinthians 15:3–6).

He Is the Only Way to God
"Jesus said to him, 'I am the way, and the truth, and the life; no one comes to the Father but through Me'" (John 14:6).

This diagram illustrates that God has bridged the chasm that separates us from Him by sending His Son, Jesus Christ, to die on the cross in our place to pay the penalty for our sins.

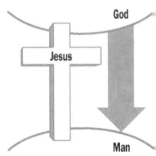

It is not enough to know these three laws...

Law Four

WE MUST INDIVIDUALLY **RECEIVE** JESUS CHRIST AS SAVIOR AND LORD; THEN WE CAN KNOW AND EXPERIENCE GOD'S LOVE AND PLAN FOR OUR LIVES.

We Must Receive Christ

"As many as received Him, to them He gave the right to become children of God, even to those who believe in His name" (John 1:12).

We Receive Christ Through Faith

"By grace you have been saved through faith; and that not of yourselves, it is the gift of God; not as a result of works that no one should boast" (Ephesians 2:8, 9).

When We Receive Christ, We Experience a New Birth

(Read John 3:1–8.)

We Receive Christ Through Personal Invitation

[Christ speaking] "Behold, I stand at the door and knock; if any one hears My voice and opens the door, I will come in to him" (Revelation 3:20).

Receiving Christ involves turning to God from self (repentance) and trusting Christ to come into our lives to forgive our sins and to make us what He wants us to be. Just to agree intellectually that Jesus Christ is the Son of God and that He died on the cross for our sins is not enough. Nor is it enough to have an emotional experience. We receive Jesus Christ by faith, as an act of the will.

These two circles represent two kinds of lives:

Self-Directed Life
S - Self is on the throne
† - Christ is outside the life
● - Interests are directed by self, often resulting in discord and frustration

Christ-Directed Life
† - Christ is in the life and on the throne
S - Self is yielding to Christ
● - Interests are directed by Christ, resulting in harmony with God's plan

Which circle best represents your life?

Which circle would you like to have represent your life?

The following explains how you can receive Christ:

YOU CAN RECEIVE CHRIST RIGHT NOW BY FAITH THROUGH PRAYER

(Prayer is talking with God)

God knows your heart and is not so concerned with your words as He is with the attitude of your heart. The following is a suggested prayer:

Lord Jesus, I need You. Thank You for dying on the cross for my sins. I open the door of my life and receive You as my Savior and Lord. Thank You for forgiving my sins and giving me eternal life. Take control of the throne of my life. Make me the kind of person You want me to be.

Does this prayer express the desire of your heart?

If it does, pray this prayer right now, and Christ will come into your life, as He promised.

How to Know That Christ Is in Your Life

Did you receive Christ into your life? According to His promise in Revelation 3:20, where is Christ right now in relation to you?

Christ said that He would come into your life. Would He mislead you? On what authority do you know that God has answered your prayer? (The trustworthiness of God Himself and His Word.)

The Bible Promises Eternal Life to All Who Receive Christ

"The witness is this, that God has given us eternal life, and this life is in His Son. He who has the Son has the life; he who does not have the Son of God does not have the life. These things I have written to you who believe in the name of the Son of God, in order that you may know that you have eternal life" (1 John 5:11–13).

Thank God often that Christ is in your life and that He will never leave you (Hebrews 13:5). You can know on the basis of His promise that the living Christ indwells you and that you have eternal life from the very moment you invite Him in. He will not deceive you.

Resources to Help You Study

Transferable Concepts. Exciting tools to help you experience and share the abundant Christian life. These booklets explain the "how-to's" of consistent, successful Christian living. Use for personal study, follow-up, and discipling others.

How You Can Be Sure You Are a Christian
Resource for Lesson 1

How You Can Experience God's Love and Forgiveness
Resource for Lesson 2

How You Can Be Filled With the Holy Spirit
Resource for Lesson 3

How You Can Walk in the Spirit
Resource for Lesson 4

How You Can Be a Fruitful Witness
Resource for Lesson 5

How You Can Introduce Others to Christ
Resource for Lesson 5

How You Can Help Fulfill the Great Commission

How You Can Love By Faith

How You Can Pray With Confidence
Resource for Lesson 5

How You Can Experience the Adventure of Giving

How You Can Study the Bible Effectively

Ten Basic Steps. A comprehensive curriculum for the Christian who wants to master the basics of Christian growth. Used by hundreds of thousands worldwide. Study Guides and Leader's Guide available.

Study Guides: Eleven individual booklets

Introduction: The Uniqueness of Jesus

Step 1: The Christian Adventure
Resource for Lesson 1

Step 2: The Christian and the Abundant Life

Step 3: The Christian and the Holy Spirit
Resource for Lesson 3

Step 4: The Christian and Prayer

Step 5: The Christian and the Bible

Step 6: The Christian and Obedience

Step 7: The Christian and Witnessing
Resource for Lesson 5

Step 8: The Christian and Giving

Step 9: Exploring the Old Testament

Step 10: Exploring the New Testament

Leader's Guide: The ultimate resource for those who want to lead a Bible Study. Contains study outlines, questions and answers from the Study Guide, and leader's instructions for teaching the complete series. An easy-to-use guide for even the most inexperienced, timid person asked to lead a group study.

A Handbook for Christian Maturity: Combines the entire series of the Ten Basic Steps in one volume. A handy resource for private or group Bible study. An excellent book to help nurture spiritual growth and maturity, this time-tested handbook has helped millions around the world discover the secret of the abundant life.

A Man Without Equal (VHS/DVD). Intriguing 30-minute video explores the uniqueness of Jesus through dramatic recreations and breath-taking portraits from the great Masters. An effective evangelism tool, giving viewers an opportunity to receive Christ. Excellent for Sunday school, group meetings, or personal study. This video can be used to help start your Five Steps group.

A Man Without Equal (book). A fresh look at the unique birth, teachings, death, and resurrection of Jesus and how He continues to change the way we live and think. Excellent as an evangelistic tool. Readers are given an opportunity to receive Christ.

Life Without Equal. Discover purpose, peace, and power for living. A presentation of the length and breadth of the Christian's freedom in Jesus Christ and how believers can release Christ's' resurrection power for life and ministry. Good for unbelievers or Christians who want to grow in their Christian life. *Resource for Lesson 5*

Four Spiritual Laws booklet (pkg. of 25). One of the most effective evangelistic tools ever developed. An easy-to-use way of sharing your faith with others. An estimated 1.5 billion copies have been distributed in all major languages.

Would You Like to Know God Personally? booklet (pkg. of 25). An adaptation of the Four Spiritual Laws. Presents four principles for establishing a personal relationship with God through Jesus Christ.

Spirit-Filled Life booklet (pkg. of 25). Discover the reality of the Spirit-filled life and how to live in moment-by-moment dependence on Him.

The Secret. An inspiring book showing you how to discover a new dimension of happiness and joy in your Christian walk and draw upon the purpose, power, and guidance of the Holy Spirit.

Witnessing Without Fear. A step-by-step guide to sharing your faith with confidence. Ideal for both individual and group study. A Gold Medallion winner.

Resources available through Campus Crusade for Christ at 1-800-827-2788 or www.campuscrusade.org.

BILL BRIGHT was the founder and president of Campus Crusade for Christ International, the world's largest Christian ministry which serves people in 191 countries through a staff of 26,000 full-time employees and more than 225,000 trained volunteers.

Dr. Bright did graduate studies at Princeton and Fuller Theological seminaries and was the recipient of five honorary doctorates as well as many national and international awards. In 1996 Bright was presented with the prestigious Templeton Prize for Progress in Religion, for his work with fasting and prayer. Worth more than $1 million, the Templeton Prize is the world's largest financial annual award. Bright donated all of his prize money to causes promoting the spiritual benefits of fasting and prayer.

In 2000, Bright received the first Lifetime Achievement Award from his alma mater, Northeastern State University. In that same year, Bright and his wife were given the Lifetime Inspiration Award from Religious Heritage of America Foundation. Additionally, he received the Lifetime Achievement Award from both the National Association of Evangelicals and the Evangelical Christian Publishers Association. In 2002, Dr. Bright was inducted into the National Religious Broadcasters Hall of Fame. He authored over 100 books and publications committed to helping fulfill the Great Commission.

Before Dr. Bright went home to be with the Lord on July 19, 2003, he established Bright Media Foundation to promote and extend his written legacy to future generations.